Doodle
and Draw
Spots,
Stripes,
and
Squiggles

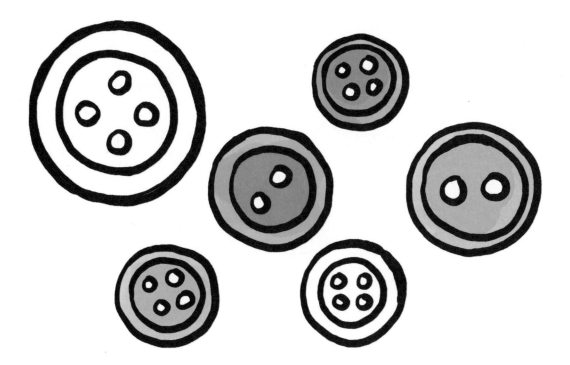

This edition published by Parragon Books Ltd in 2014 and distributed by

Parragon Inc.
440 Park Avenue South, 13th Floor
New York, NY 10016
www.parragon.com

Written by Susan Fairbrother   Illustrated by Bella Bee and Mike Garton

ISBN 978-1-4723-6497-5

Printed in China

Doodle
and Draw
Spots,
Stripes,
and
Squiggles

PaRRagon

Bath · New York · Cologne · Melbourne · Delhi
Hong Kong · Shenzhen · Singapore · Amsterdam

Finish the line patterns.

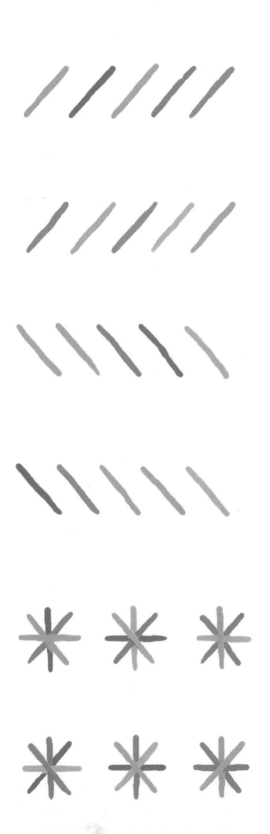

Use your patterns for rain and snow.

Trace some web patterns, then add spiders.

Try out some swirls.

Color this sea creature pattern by dots!

Doodle a cloud pattern.

Draw a star
pattern in the
night sky.

Trace the Lines to make a spiky, zigzag pattern!

Trace the lines to make a curly, swirly pattern!

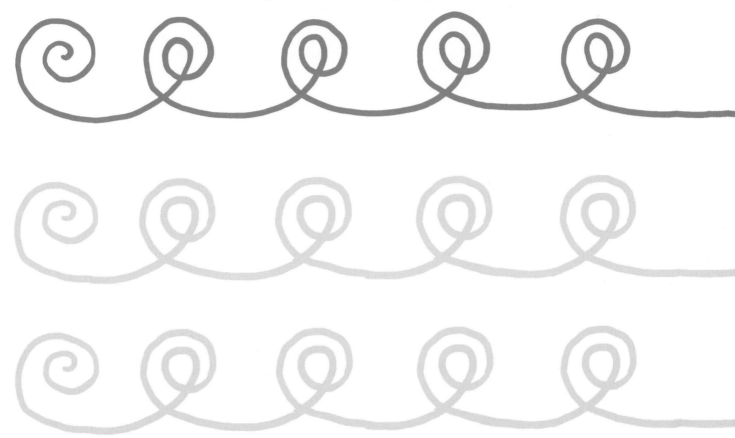

Finish the brick pattern with rectangles.

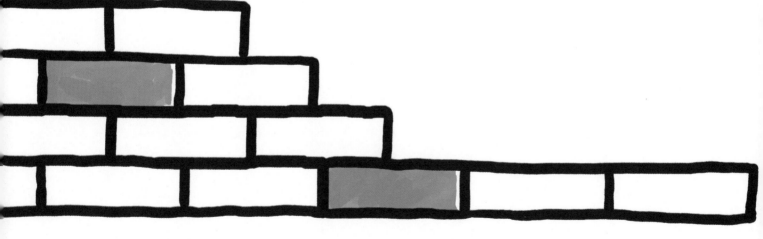

caterpillar counting!

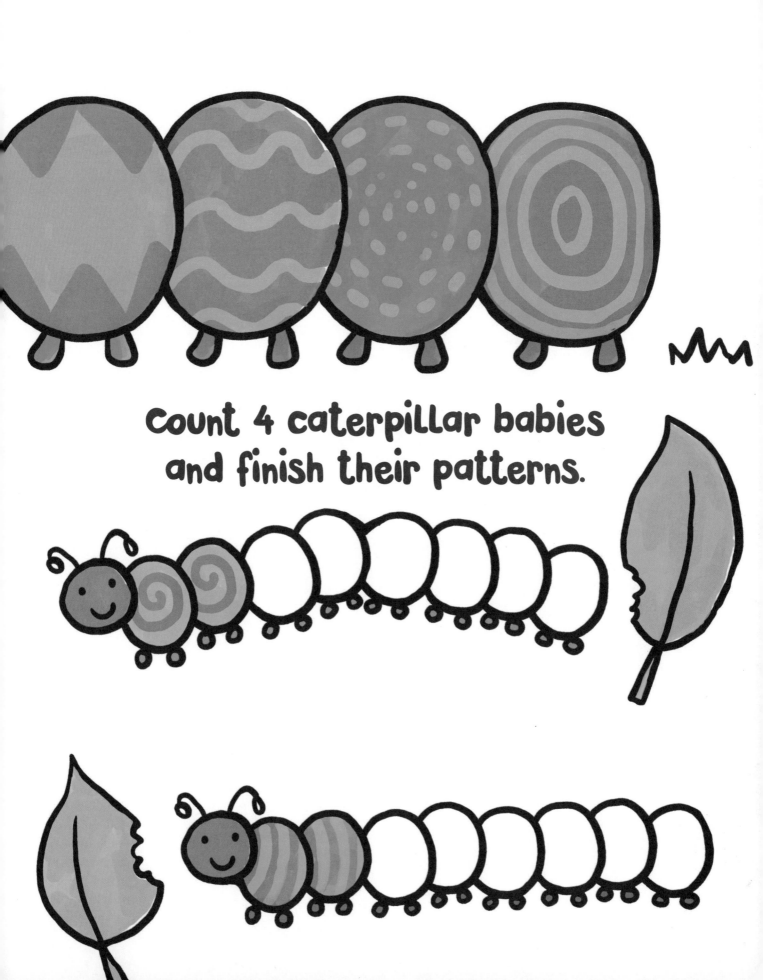

count 4 caterpillar babies
and finish their patterns.

Add more circle patterns.

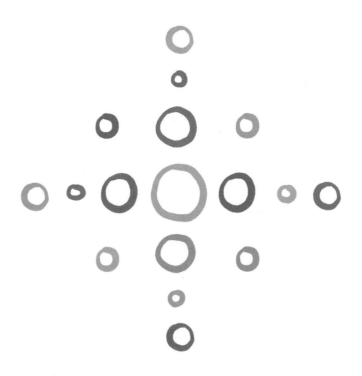

Complete the rainbow patterns!

Gloves and mittens.
Make some woolly patterns!

finish the shell patterns.

10 silly snakes ... give them all stripes!

Try a swirl.

Try a fan.

Doodle more squares and rectangles.

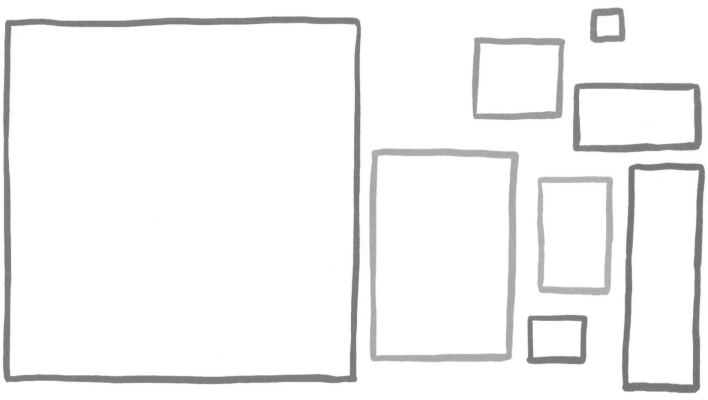

They all have 4 sides.

Add a pattern of squares to this robot.

cupcakes, yum!

Add swirl and sprinkle patterns.

Finish the zigzag patterns.

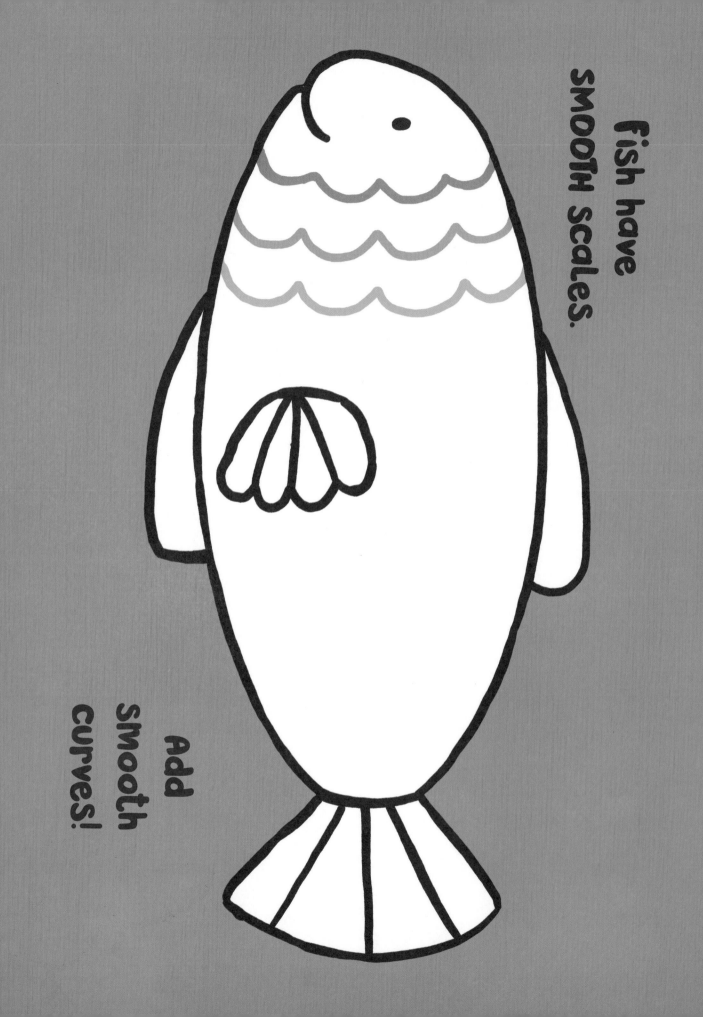

Fish have SMOOTH SCALES.

Add smooth curves!

Crocodiles have spiky scales.
Add zigzags!

Finish each sun with circles or triangles to make them all shine!

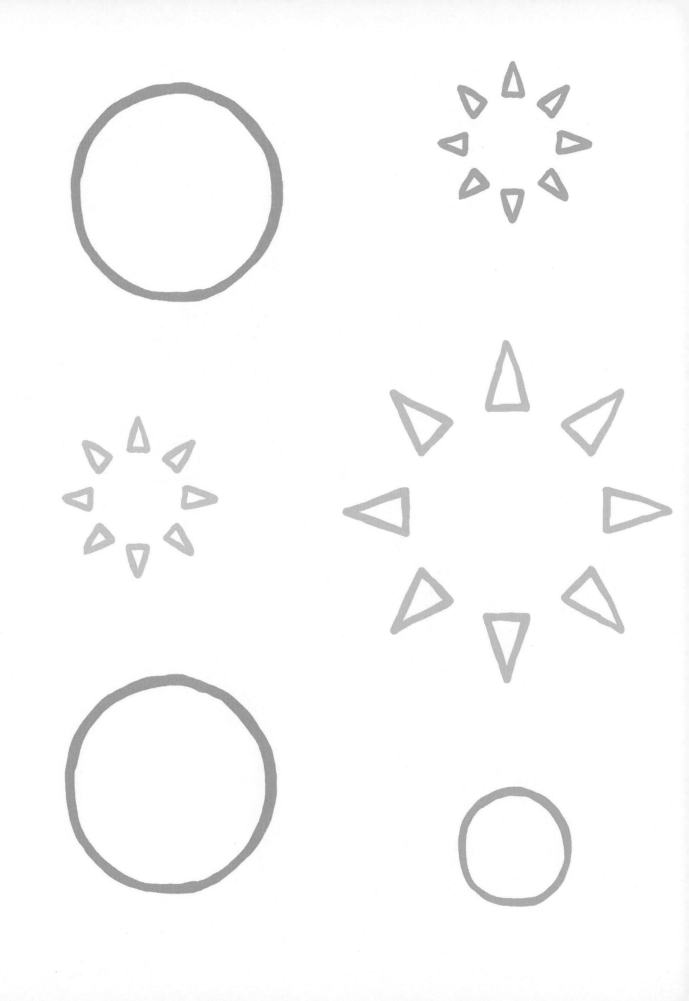

5 furry squirrels.

Finish the patterns on each tail.

Raindrop patterns.
Add some more to make it pour!

Wavy patterns.
Add more wiggly Lines.

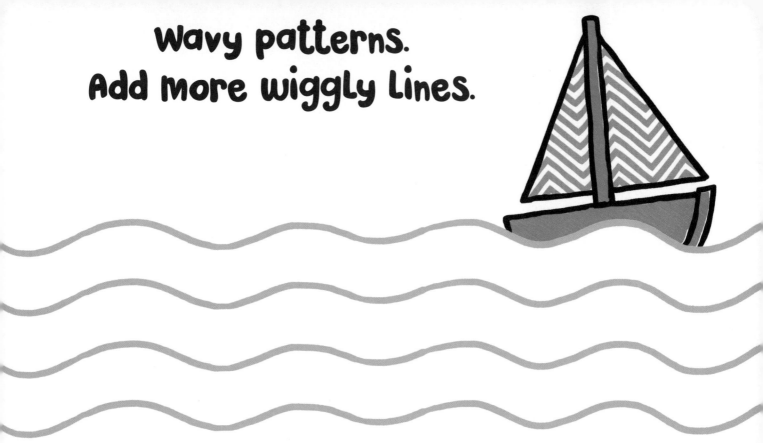

Give every bird a pattern.

Count 5 little red birds.

Tweet, tweet!

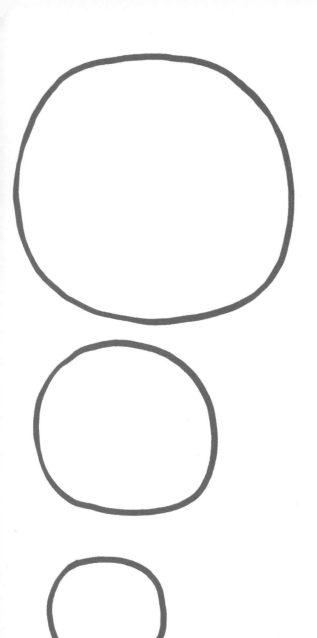

Someone's been shaking the bottles of soda.

Add more BIG and SMALL bubbles.

What a beautiful blanket, Bear!

color a pattern in each square.

Finish the patterns on each pretty dress.

Add triangles to each train to complete the patterns.

Try curls and swirls.

Give Bear a big curly hairdo.

Pineapples!
special offer!

Fill the pineapples
with patterns.

who's watching the game?

Add faces and colors to the crowd pattern.

Rabbit is redecorating.

Complete the
wallpaper patterns.

FiLL in the missing shapes.

Extraordinary elephants!

finish coloring the pattern.

Wool Shop

Try some scribble balls.

Draw 3 pink balls.

Draw 4 green balls.

Add more red balls.

what is Rabbit knitting?

Draw something and fill it with a woolly pattern.

Draw straight Lines for Leaves.

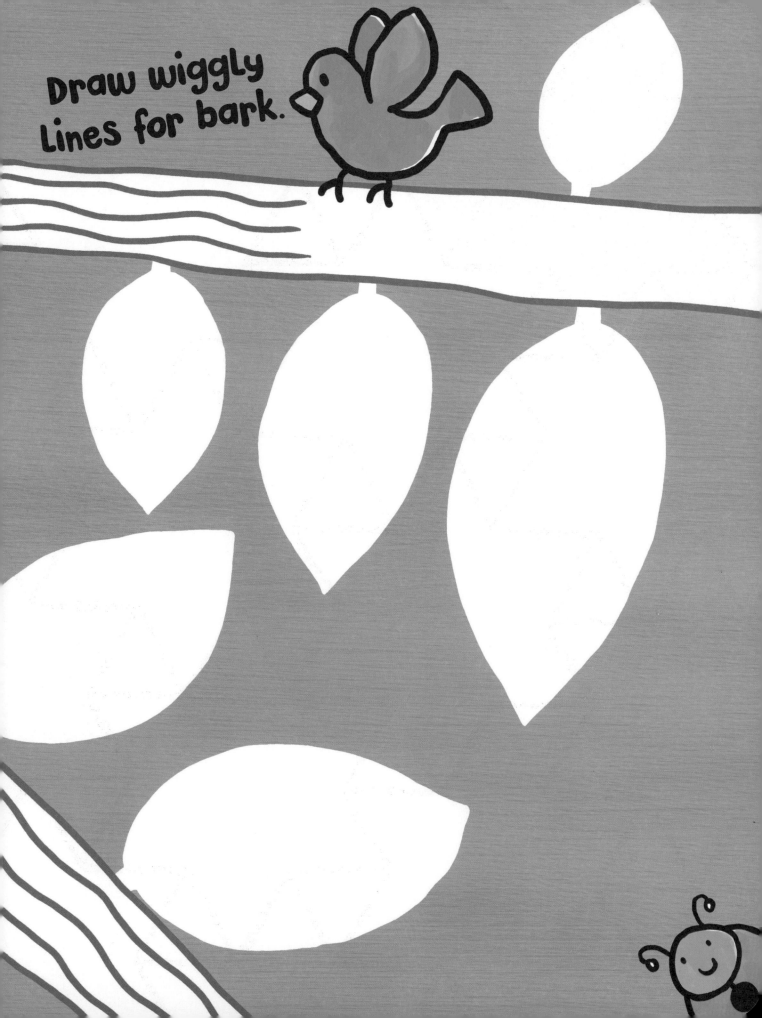

Draw wiggly lines for bark.

color the pattern.

Finish the squiggles.

Wheeee!

Add squiggles
to make
the cat
extra furry!

Puppies love puddles!

Add blobs to make
a puddly pattern!

Can-you-create-a-saurus?

Give them all scaly patterns.

stomp, stomp, stomp!

What colorful patterns will you add to the hats?

Finish the check pattern by coloring the squares.

Color the checks on the shirts.

shaggy dogs! finish their hairy patterns.

Give him a wavy pattern.

Give him a zigzag pattern.

Turn this pattern into friendly fish!

Make a pattern with as many bubbles as you can!

Decorate the plain sails with patterns.

Shh! The owls are sleeping.
Finish their feather patterns.

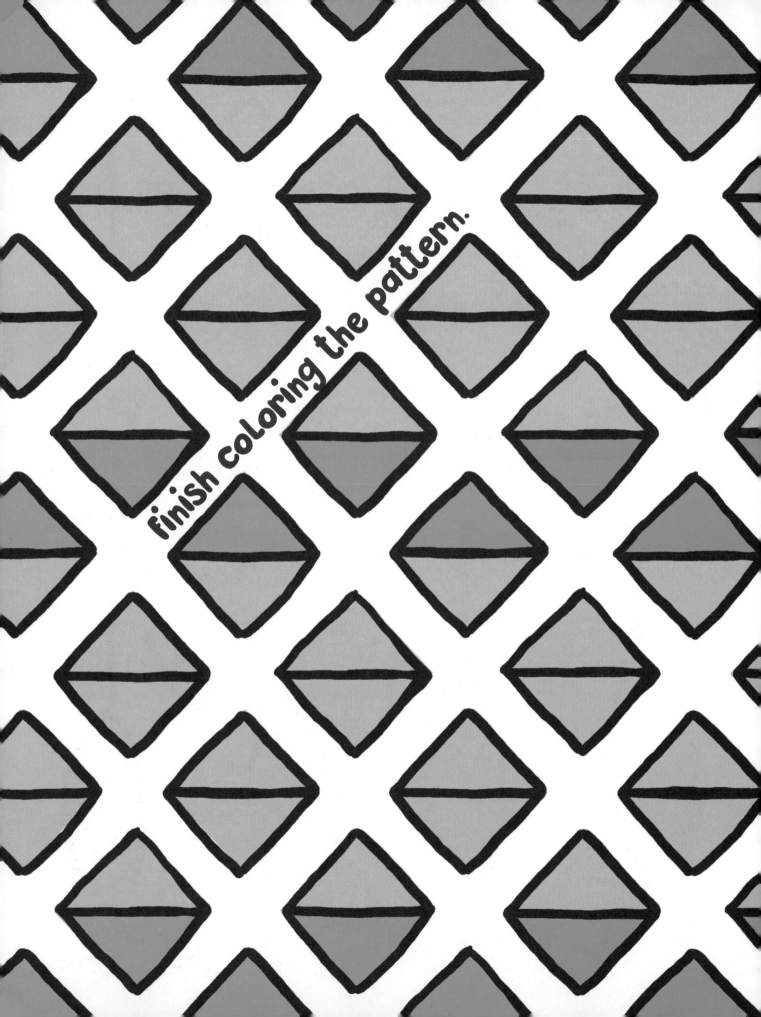

finish coloring the pattern.

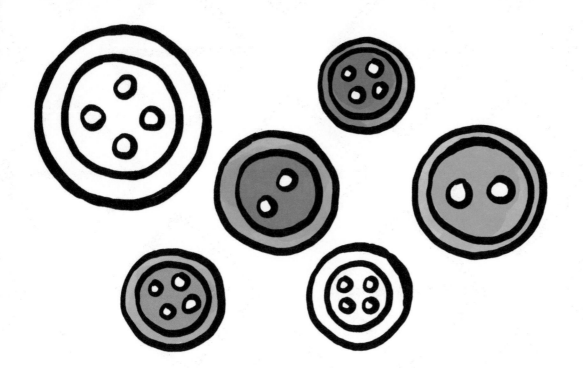

Fill the page with a big
button pattern.

These porcupines should all be very spiky!

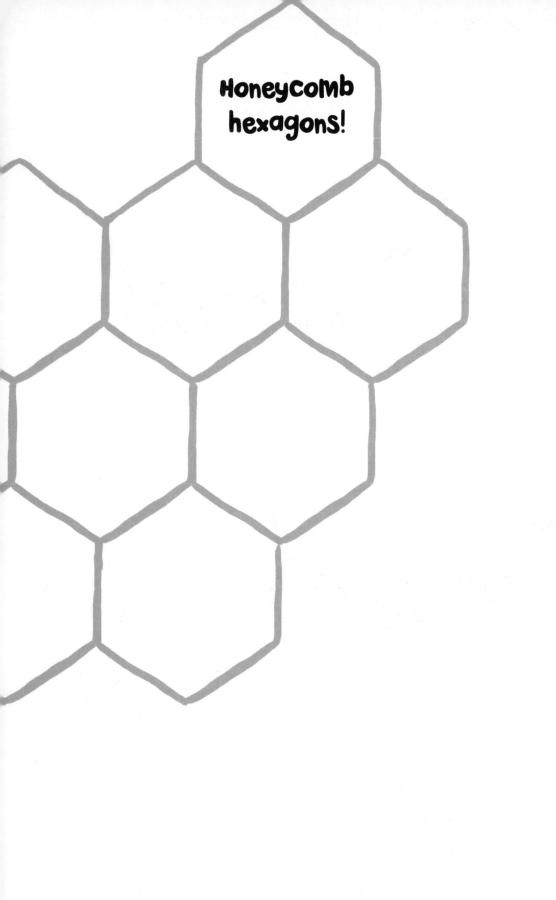

Honeycomb hexagons!

Make all the bees stripy.

circles make perfect flowers.

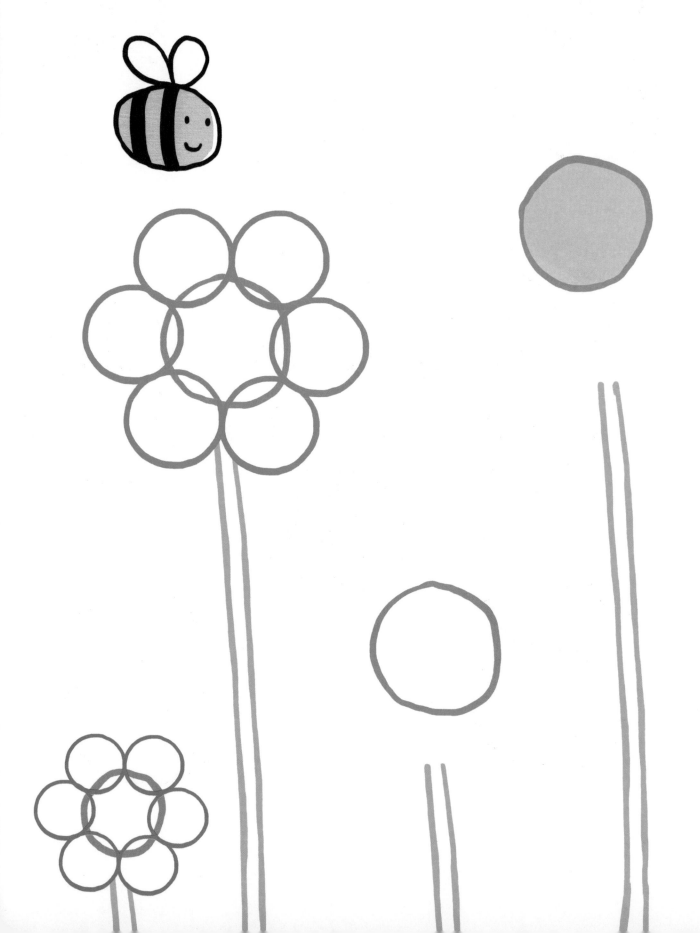

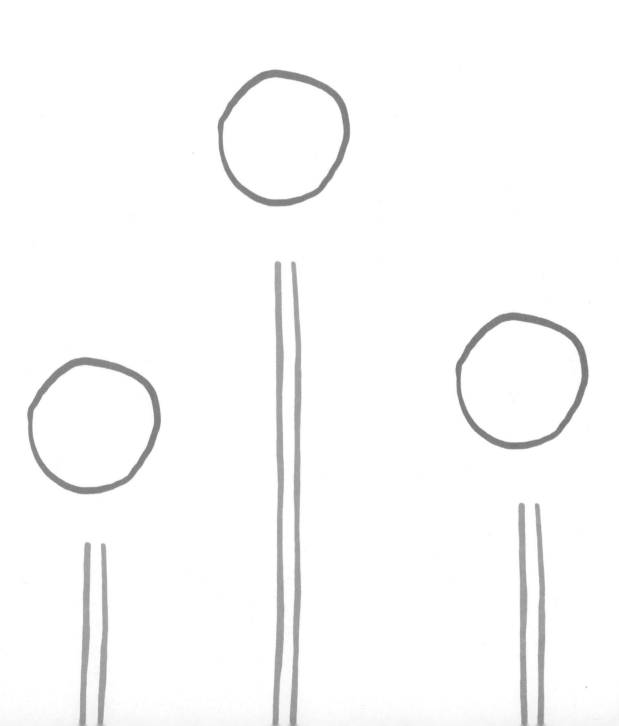

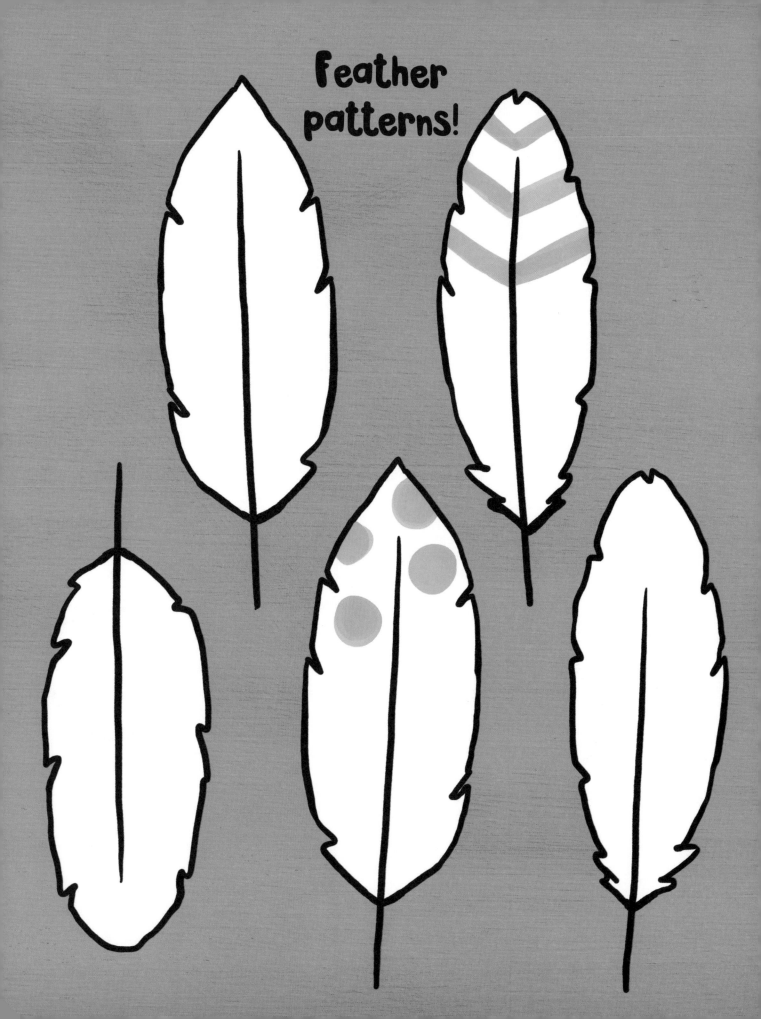

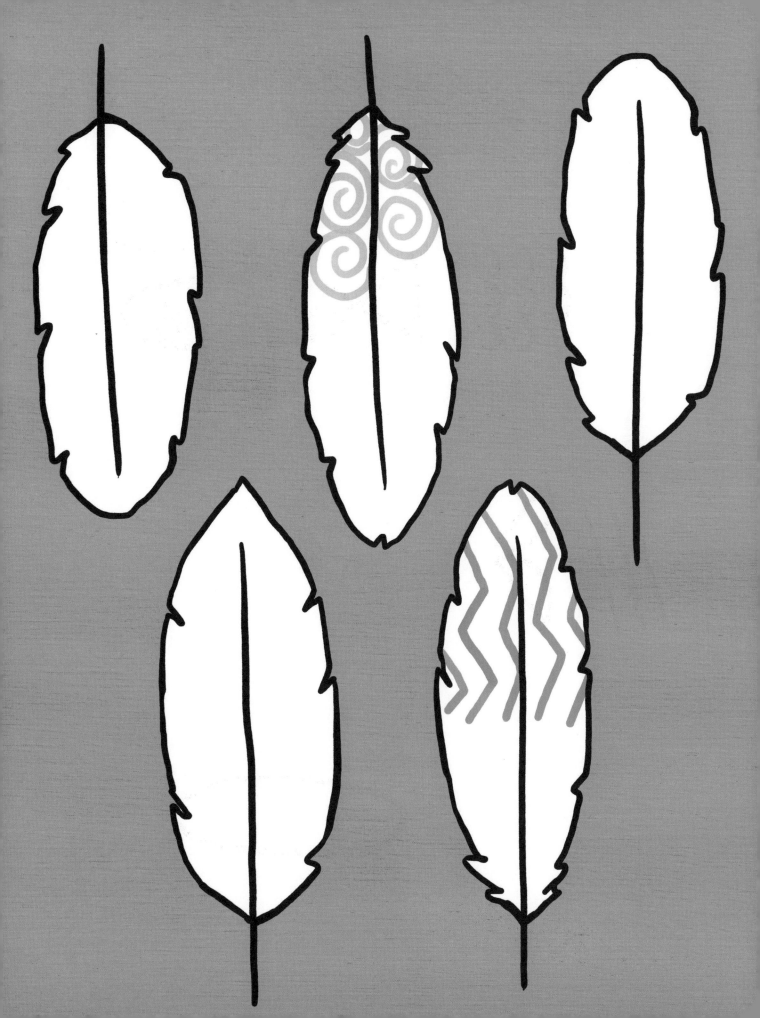

Put shapes and patterns together to make fish!

Add lines and zigzags to give every lion a magnificent mane.

Make a hand pattern.

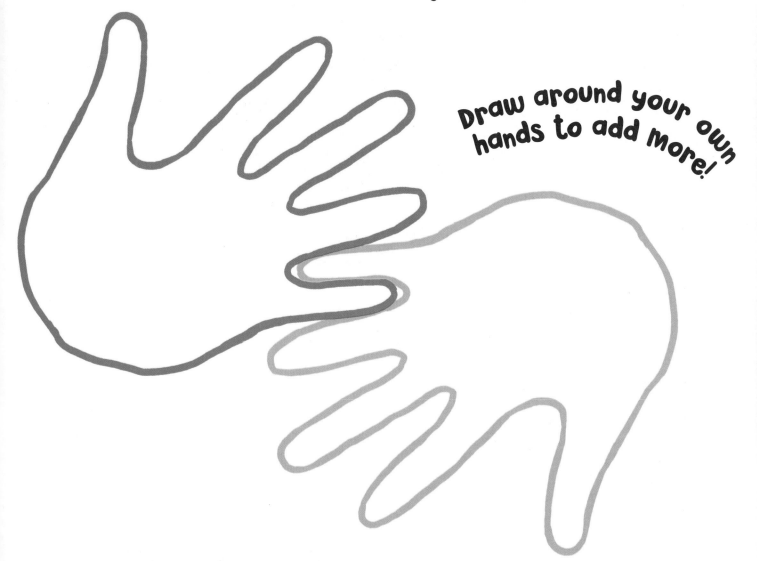

Draw around your own hands to add more!

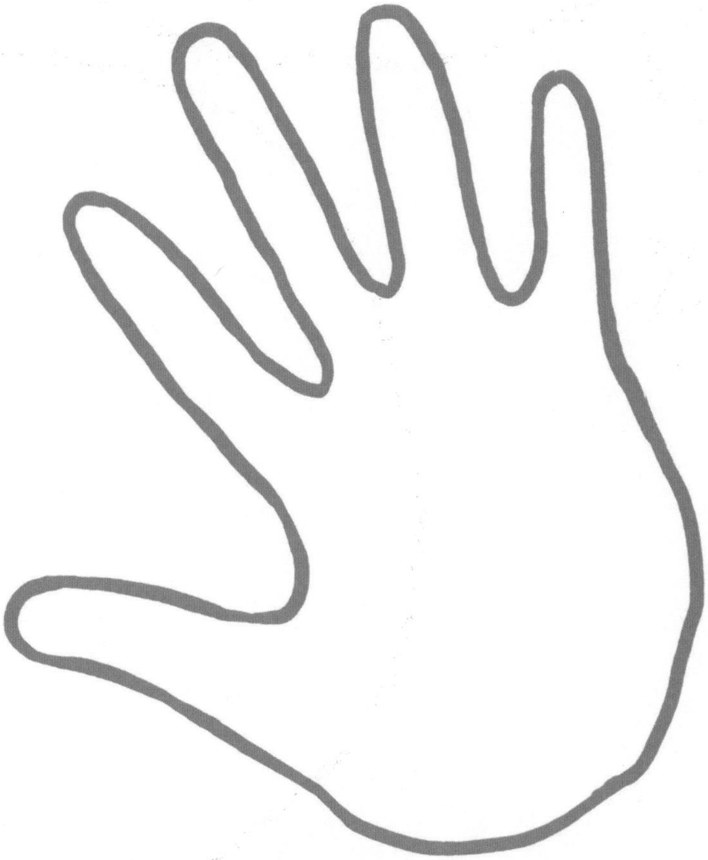

pattern planets.

Finish the tire track patterns.

Turn this pattern into colorful penguins!

Count 20 animals!

Give them all a pattern.

Delicious!

Decorate the
donuts with
patterns.

yum!

Colorful
woollies!
Add patterns
to the scarves
and hats.